I'm Hans Christian Andersen premi
Edinburgh in August 2010. It was a
Wall and the Pleasance, directed l
and performed by Rachel Rose Rei

The production received glowing praise in the British press, and subsequently toured nationally and internationally.

Praise for I'm Hans Christian Andersen:

'Rachel Rose Reid is a young contemporary storyteller of immense skill and breathless conviction...there's no faulting Reid's command of her craft.'
Donald Hutera, The Times

'polished and compelling...a consummate performer, definitely one to watch.'
Alice Jones, The Independent

'Reid's approach is so personal, idiosyncratic and unpredictable... It's like Peter Schaffer reimagining Mozart – an artistic life retold, as the vehicle for another artist's ideas and preoccupations. It's marvellous.'
Corinne Salisbury, British Theatre Guide

'...an ideal mix of wit, humour and emotion ... in this brilliant show, Reid connects us with our universal search for the happy ending and the pressure that we all put on ourselves to get things "right".'
Emma Osment, Litro Magazine

'A lesson in the power of a good story creatively told... astonishing.'
The Canberra Times

I'm Hans Christian Andersen

Rachel Rose Reid

Burning Eye

BurningEyeBooks
Never Knowingly
Mainstream

This edition published by Burning Eye Books 2021

www.burningeye.co.uk

@burningeyebooks

Burning Eye Books
15 West Hill, Portishead, BS20 6LG

ISBN 978-9-913958-08-4

www.rachelrosereid.com
@rachelrosereid

Rachel Rose Reid, *'Queen of the New Wave of Storytellers'* (Ian McMillan, BBC Radio) blends traditional storytelling with contemporary spoken word. Since writing *I'm Hans Christian Andersen,* she has toured her work internationally, from the Nuyorican Poets Café to the Soho Theatre, and has collaborated and created commissions for a characteristically eclectic range of partners including Billy Bragg, London City Sinfonia, Dickens' Bicentenary (as Writer in Residence), BBC Radio 3, and Old Vic, New Voices.

For Stella

There is a place…
Far out on the ocean the waves are as blue as the loveliest cornflowers and as clear as glass, and you mustn't think there's no one down there. No! There in the deep is where the mermaids live.

And the little mermaid falls in love with the handsome prince, but he lives up there in the castle, and she is down here in the depths of the ocean. So she goes to the ugly witch of the sea to exchange her beautiful voice for the chance to have feet and legs and to be with him.
"If in three days you can acquire eternal love with him," the witch says, "then you shall live happily ever after, but if you fail you will be turned into foam on the ocean waves."

But it's okay, because Sebastian the lobster sings a happy song, and Flounder the little fish whistles a merry tune, and good wins over evil and the witch is destroyed, and the mermaid gets her man. And her feet. And her legs. And the pair sail off.
That's the mermaid and the prince, not the legs.
Well, obviously the legs, but—

Anyway, the pair sail off into eternal love and Happily Ever After.

That's the Disney version.

Anyone know the original ending?

Anyone?
Ah well.

We have plenty of time for endings later.
We've only just begun!

Let's start again shall we?

I'm Hans Christian Andersen

Rachel Rose Reid

Burning Eye

Hans Christian Andersen. We all know him. Jolly journeyman shoemaker! Danny Kaye singing *Inchworm* to the rosy-cheeked children whilst the schoolmaster runs down the lane shouting, "Bring back them kids!"

Yes?

No?

That's the Disney version too.

Let's start again shall we?

I'm Hans Christian Andersen

Rachel Rose Reid

Burning Eye

Let's begin. When we get to the end we'll know more than we know now.

Here we are, ready for our journey: the open book, the fresh white page, the life as yet unwritten.

We begin.

Where should a fairy tale begin?

We begin in a castle surrounded by fresh water, which laps cold at the thick stone walls and ripples back reflecting the yellow light of an early spring dawn.

All is hushed, doors are shut, curtains drawn, gates are locked.

The Lady of the castle ushers a servant into a brocaded bed-chamber and says, "Put the hot water and the towels down here."

On the soft duck-down coverlet, breathing heavily, lies a beautiful young princess (who else?). The sun has pulled its chariot almost fully through the sky, and is turning for the forest on the distant hill by the time she has given birth. A baby boy with pale white skin and pea green eyes. She holds him to her breast, passes him up to the waiting arms of the lady, and turns away.

Countess Severin lifts the wiped-clean child into her arms. This is the firstborn grandson of Frederick the 4th, the first born son of this woman lying here and Christian the 8th, heir to the Throne of Denmark. They are not married.

So this is a tale that cannot be told; the first page ripped out and a fresh story begun before even a chapter is written.

With a vow of secrecy on her lips, Countess Severin's maid-servant steps out over the bridge, water shuckling beneath her in the silver moonlight.

Anne Marie Andersen carries that bundle all the way home, shushing and cooing, tempering his wails with lullabies. From the sweet scent of forest flowers to new smells.

Fish rotting in the gutters, the river clogged with dirt. Ducks and chickens scatter in her wake as she crushes egg-shells beneath her feet in her hurry to get home.

As the red rim of dawn lines the horizon she steps over the threshold of her own home in the slums. She places the baby down in the palm of the bed. Now the sun spins back up through the trees, startling the birds into song.

It is April the 2nd, eighteen hundred and five.
Anne Marie names her new child
Hans Christian Andersen.

Is it true?

What can I tell you?
The only things we have left of Andersen – or anyone – are the stories written and the stories told.

And why these stories?
Why am I here with the stories he told?

I will tell you.

I had wiped Andersen's stories from my memory almost entirely and then, about eighteen months ago, I was at the start of a new relationship. This is relevant. I was at the start of a new relationship and I was sitting in my kitchen, waiting for the phone to ring. On the radio I heard a woman talking about Hans Christian Andersen.

She said that Andersen was in his thirties when he wrote his first major fairytale, that he wrote The Little Mermaid whilst staying on an island to the East of Denmark, avoiding the wedding of the person he loved.

I thought, "that doesn't sound like a story that involves singing lobsters."

So I picked his book out from my shelf. I sat down at the table. I opened it. I began to read, and as I read the stories, I remembered when I'd first heard them.
Do you know how that is?
You open one memory and a thousand more pour out.

I was 5 years old.

I remember sitting next to a boy in nursery, and the grown ups said we spent so much time together that he was a Boyfriend and I was a Girlfriend.
That he was my Prince.
That we would get married.
That he was my First Love.

We sat hand in hand in the corner of the classroom.

The teacher sat high up on her chair and she opened the old book of fairytales and she read...

There is a place.
A grand house.
In the house there is a room, and in the room there is a table, and on the table there were two china figurines: a blonde and dainty shepherdess, and a tiny chimney sweep.

And although she looked delicate and he looked shabby, they were actually made from the same stuff. And because they had been set down together, and because they were made from the same stuff, they decided to fall in love, get married, and live happily ever after.

But a third figurine stood next to them, an old Chinese nobleman. And he said that he was the shepherdess's grandfather, which meant that he could tell her who to marry. He said, "You shall marry the man on the cupboard door, on the other side of the room."

You know those cupboards? Dark wood, with flowers and foliage carved into them? On this one, there was a man. He had horns on his head, a smirk on his face, and where his feet should be he had shaggy goat hooves, so the children who came into the parlour called him Mr. Sergeant Major General Goaty-Legs.

"With a title like that," said her grandfather, "he is the one for you!"
"I don't want to live in a cupboard," she said.
But grandfather wasn't listening.
"You will marry him tonight!" He said, and he fell asleep.

In the dark the shepherdess wept and cried out to her lover. "We can't stay here," she said, "I don't love him, I love you! We must escape. Will you come with me?"

"I will do anything for you," he said, "I love you too. Yes, I can support you with my profession. Let's go. Let's escape! Let's run away! Let's leave this place and be free!"

"If only we could move," said the china shepherdess.

"Do you trust me?" said the sweep.

He held out his hand.

How very enviously all the other figurines in the room stretched and strained their necks from where they were set, as they watched the sweep and shepherdess slide down the gilded table leg and across the wooden floor.

"Get them!" cried her grandfather.

"Get them!" cried Sergeant Major General Goaty-Legs.

So they ran as fast as they could, slipping and sliding over the French polished boards and jumped – plop! – into a drawer.

In the drawer they found themselves surrounded by playing cards – the jacks, kings, queens and jokers – all watching a play being performed by the puppet theatre. Oh, it was a beautiful play in that black box, I wish you could have seen it. It was about two lovers who couldn't be together, which made the shepherdess cry because it reminded her of her own life.

"We can't stay here," she said. "We must go further. Let's go out into the Big Wide World".

The sweep looked into her painted blue eyes.

He said, "I can show you the way to the Big Wide World, but have you really thought about it enough? Do you know how difficult it is to get there? What a hard journey it will be, and how, once we get there, everything will change? We can never come back."
"Yes!" she said.
She held out her hand.

So, they went the way a chimney sweep knows. Out of the drawer, through the grate of the stove, through its belly, inside the pipe and up into the chimney. Can you imagine the determination it takes for two such tiny figures to climb up an enormous chimney, as the brickwork chips and scratches at their paint and porcelain?
"Look!" he said, "the loveliest star is shining."
Higher and higher they scrabbled breathlessly until, at last, with a puff of soot, they were on top of the house, at the edge of the world.

There were the rooftops below, the stars above, and the Big Wide World ahead of them, far and out of sight.
"We've made it," cried the sweep, and he did a little celebration dance.

She wasn't dancing.

The shepherdess was looking out at the world. In all her wildest dreams she had never imagined it would be quite this Big.
So many stars, so many houses, so many roads, so many pathways, so many rooms, so many tables, so many sweeps.
So many shepherdesses.

"We have to go back."

"What?" he said, "but we can't go back now. We've only just begun."

He spoke to her of the tiny life they had left behind and of the infinite possibilities in the World ahead. But the more he talked, the more she cried, until all the gold came off her sash.

What choice did he have?

Gently he carried her, shaking and fragile, all the way back down the chimney, across the floor, up onto the table top. When they looked down, they saw grandfather had smashed into pieces, so now there was no one to tell them whom to marry.

"Oh," sighed the shepherdess, "What a journey."

"Yes," said the sweep, "look how far we've come."

So, the sweep and the shepherdess – because they were made from the same stuff, because they had been set down together – decided to fall in love and get married. They stood on the same tabletop for the rest of their lives, and they loved each other until they broke.

I remember walking back from nursery that day.

My mum said "Now, don't get too excited, but we're moving home!"

"Where to?" I said, "to a castle with my Prince?"

"No," she said, "Slough."

All the grown ups who had played make-believe with me felt they should tell me the truth before I left.

My neighbour said, "You know I told you there are fairies at the bottom of my garden?"

I said, "Yes! Can I take one with me?"

He said, "No. They don't exist."

My best friend's mum said, "You know I told you there's a magical world you can climb to through the cupboard door in our bathroom?"

I said, "Yes can we visit it before I go?"

She said, "Yes." She held out her hand, and we climbed up the stairs, and we walked into the bathroom, and she stretched out her arm, and she opened the door and I looked inside and it was full of towels.

And I didn't see my Prince again.

On the radio the woman said we don't know if Andersen knew that he might secretly be a Danish prince, but we do know that he thought there was more to his destiny than making shoes.

At 14 years old he left the slums of Odense for the big wide world.

He made a name for himself going from door-to-wealthy-door, writing one-boy Shakespeare plays that were met with gales of laughter. He boldly entered the houses of famous poets and writers, persuading them to become his patrons and mentors. Somehow he got a grant for his education from the King.

All of which reminded me that at 14 years old, I was getting minimum wage from the Slough High Street branch of Café Rouge.
Polishing the forks, I thought, "there must be more to life than this."
So, I bought a notebook and I had a think.

MEMO BOOK

By the age of 25, Andersen was scraping at the underside of the highest echelons of Danish society.

In the light of a crackling fire a silk-lined family sit to read the latest writings they've received.

The older gentleman declares, "His stories really have improved." The young woman nods eagerly.

The young man fixes his steel-blue eyes to the page and agrees.

They look out into the black, and await the visitor.

Amber lanterns reflect in the harbour ice. The passenger can see through the frosted carriage window how every house is aglow, as parlour by parlour is lit with the light of a hundred candles on every freshly cut fir tree.

Copenhagen is trembling with anticipation for the Christmas Ball.

The carriage pulls up in front of a grand house.

The horses jangle to a stop and puff steam into the air. Out steps the young man, unfolding his long, gangling legs packed into an old suit that stops two inches above the ankle.

Hans Christian slips and slides up the flagstone steps, pulls on the cord of the bell of the house of his patron.

He has just enough time to wonder how he got here from where he began.

A servant leads him into a large room. He waits beside an enormous Christmas tree. There are pictures on the walls. Men and women. Men alone. Tall and proud like trees in a forest. Hans Christian shuts his eyes and pictures himself framed amongst them.

He turns.

There stands his patron, Jonas Collin, who holds out a leathery palm and says, "Andersen! At last! There is so much to discuss. Now, this time you must meet my children, they're about your age. Here is Louise, and here is – ah. He was here a moment ago – Edvard?"

Edvard.

There's an article I cut out of a magazine that says you can predict an entire relationship from the first minute of your encounter.

Andersen stares up at the polished door.

Whenever I'm waiting for someone, or something, that's when I write.

I don't know about you, but when I start a new notebook, whatever is on the first page has to be perfect, nothing can be crossed out or scribbled, because if the first page isn't right, it feels like the whole thing will be a mess. And it has to be some really deep thought to inspire how the rest of the book will be.

So, luckily for my first notebook, I met my first love (my first real love).

He has a husky voice, and comes all the way from Canada. In the first sixty seconds of our encounter he was dancing for a crowd of admirers, and I was enchanted.

I was 15 and he was, well, he wasn't.

I was 15 and we were in love.

He kissed me when we walked through the sunlit parks, held me safe in the shelter of his arms, and spent hours singing on the phone to me.

I felt my senses reel and my mind open.

I wanted to do more.

So I crept out of my house in the middle of the night and ran away to see him and drink Cointreau and smoke pot. He taught me Joni Mitchell songs, and told me that he met her once. Joni Mitchell.

Her songs are so full of melancholy, but somehow – do you find this? – those kind of songs open my heart far more than any lyrics about perfect love.

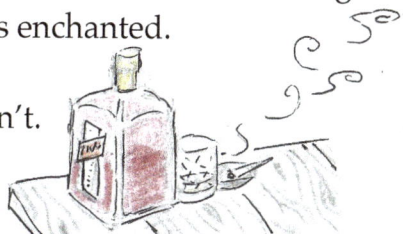

We lay down together in crisp white sheets, and I was too shy.

So, I fell asleep beside him, deeply in love, safe in the knowledge that one day my heart would just open.

Andersen stands at the stern of the ship, watches Copenhagen vanish, that familiar family waving from the quay.

He takes out his new notebook and a finely sharpened pencil.

On the first page he writes:

I am a man and yet I am still a boy. I have this abiding idea that only by being torn away from the things I love will I come to anything.

The boat slices through the glass-clear flower-blue water, the sun regaining its view of the Øresund Strait, lighting upon a letter held out by a young ship clerk. Andersen takes it. Runs his hand over the smooth wax seal, unpicks the paper from itself. He reads,

Dear Andersen,

Believe me, I am saddened by your leaving. I shall miss you dreadfully. I shall miss no longer seeing you coming up to talk to me in my rooms as usual. Yet you will miss us more, because you are alone.

Yours sincerely,

Edvard Collin

Andersen turns his face to the blue sky and blazing sun.
Inhales the exhilarating salt air.

I woke in the night.
The moon was streaming through the curtains and spilling onto the fresh white sheets.
My first love was standing over me.

Wanking.

I went into the lounge.
I think that's the bit where I was meant to leave the flat. I couldn't.
He said, "I couldn't help it, it's a guy thing."

There were a few awkward dates after that. Then it turned to nothing. Well, nearly. He called me a couple of years later.
He said, "I'm getting married!"
I think he was expecting me to be distraught, "No! Come back! Do it again! Please?"
"Congratulations," I said.
"Yeah, well," he said, "she wants to have babies and I thought, I'm in my thirties, I need to grow up."

I got my ticket, my passport, my notebook and I moved on.
I thought, if I travel far enough I will find the thing I'm looking for.

My proper, real first love.

We met in a smoky bar.

He said, "What can I get you to drink?"

I said, "I can get my own drink."

He said, "I know you can, but that's not what's happening."

Then he said, "Come with me."

And he held out his hand.

Every night we climbed up the emergency exit staircase to the roof above his flat. We looked at the rooftops below, the stars above, at the city far ahead of us.

He stood behind me and he put his arms around my waist. The heat between us melted the snow beneath my gloves and he unpeeled, unraveled, every carefully constructed layer of sugared artifice on me, and he listened.

And he wasn't pissed off with me for being slow or shy.

Perhaps it was the romance of being cocooned against the concrete. Perhaps it's because I was in another country – you know what they say about travel? – that I allowed myself to open up to him in spite of anything before.

Sitting on the bus, my friend said, "You can stay."

I said, "I want to stay."

She said, "You can stay."

I said, "No, I'm here to see the world. I can't travel all the way here just to stay in one place."

I just. I kind of. I thought that when I travelled I would find something more than a computer software engineer with a nice roof.

Hans Christian Andersen, on a tremulous May morning, with the apple blossom evident on the breeze, sits in his hotel room in Hamburg, as the carriages pull their way through the thin and winding streets beneath his window. He stares over at the garden square and back down to the empty paper flapping at him in frustration.
Shuts his eyes and thinks of Edvard Collin.

Thinks how by now Edvard will have received the package he has sent him. The three hundred page handwritten story of his life from rags to – well, nearly – to riches. Thinks how that will melt Edvard's heart.
Imagines him reading it, bursting into tears, eagerly awaiting his return. Open-mouthed, open-hearted, open-armed. Opening the door, embracing him with love. Speaking with him in familiar terms; replacing all the formality of language with the Danish form of speech reserved for friends, blood brothers, and lovers.
"Du," Edvard whispers, "Du – I will be your family now."
He kisses him.

Hans Christian imagines nights filled with sherry and cigars, Edvard laughing at his every joke.
He looks down at the page.
He writes,

Dear Edvard,

Of all people, I consider you to be my true friend. Please never cease to be that, dear Collin. I feel I can confide in you. If you want to make me truly happy – please do not be cross with me! – please can we be on 'familiar terms'. Please say 'du' to me. I would never dare to ask you in person but I can ask you now that I am away. If you refuse I shall never ask again. I shall know from the first letter you send me whether you have obliged me, and shall drink a toast to you.

You cannot imagine how my heart is pounding, although you are not here.

Yours truly,
Christian

He neatly folds the letter over twice.
Once he starts writing, maybe you know how it is, he can't seem to stop.

It all pours out.

June 1831 Cologne

...How I long for you my dear Edvard, long to speak to you from the heart and in friendship, alone up in your poetical little room.

July 1831 Paris

...I am so dearly fond of you, perhaps more than you think. With all my soul I cling to you.

August 1831 Marseille

...I never had a brother, but if I did I could not love him the way that I love you.

September 1831 Rome

...I long for you as if you were a pretty Italian girl with dark eyes.

My actual proper real first love has dark eyes, and an affinity for horror make up and false teeth, which made me shriek and giggle when he chased me around Shepherd's Bush.

And he had the idea that there's this Ideal Woman. The Ideal Woman does not tell jokes in the bath because that is inappropriate.

My genuine actual proper real first love smells of earth and country air and in the first sixty seconds of our encounter I thought he was the kind of guy that only goes for sylph-like hippy girls.

But he ran his fingers through my hair.

He pulled me into his world of herbal tea and tai chi, and down into his tent, and his hands were soft on my belly.

All is flow.

Grass rustling. Birds singing. Sun sliding through the sky above our field, and this feeling that before we – all of us – before we had schedules to work around, and weekdays to wade through, before we had dates to fit in and diaries to fill out, before we had places to get to and odd jobs to get done, our job was just being people caring for each other.

I went to stay with him in Brighton.

Where else would he live?

When his grip loosened on my hand I said, "What's wrong?" He said, "Usually I take my spirulina everyday at eight o'clock but I missed taking it because you're here, so my day's messed up now."

There's a sound in the air, like a hundred doors slamming at once with supernatural power. Andersen runs out through the streets of Naples. Vesuvius is erupting!
One side of the mountain is a river of flowing fire and the lava rolls down like falling stars. *My soul is full of love,* he writes and swoons into his room.
A letter on his bed.

He fumbles to open it, fingers slipping over the familiar seal. He reads:

Dear Andersen,

I wish to display my disposition regarding being on familiar terms with you.
As a poet I am sure you know human nature can be strange.
When you invite me to say 'du' to you this inexplicable and unpleasant feeling arises in me, like the sound of nails scraping on glass.
Why should we make this change in our relationship? Is it to give an outward sign to others? Surely our relationship is of mutual comfort and benefit. Our relationship is fine as it is. Let us speak no more of it.

Yours sincerely,

Edvard Collin

Sitting in my kitchen.
Radio resurfacing.
I put the book down.
A couple of hours had passed.
Phone still hadn't rung.
I set the kettle to boil, and flicked through an old pile of magazines.

How Do You Know They're the One?

How Much Should You Sacrifice For Love?

How Romantic Films Are Ruining Our Love Lives!

Apparently, people who watch romantic comedies expect their lovers to know what they're thinking.
I looked at the phone.
I made myself a cup of tea.
I went back to my book of fairy tales.

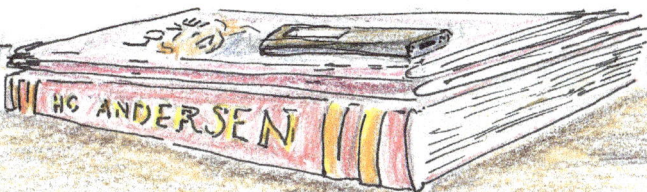

The young man wrote books.
He wrote books about what was good in the world, what was beautiful, and what was true.

He lived in the lands of the North, and there he found he had to stay inside all day because it was so cold.
He decided it would be a good idea to travel.
He travelled to the lands of the South.
There he found he had to stay inside all day because it was so hot.
Sitting, perspiring over his papers, the young man did not feel like a glamorous writer. He felt more like a chicken roasting in an oven.

But at night, things came to life.
When the young man stepped out on to the balcony,

people poured out onto the street below. Tinkers, tailors, traders, set up stalls. Tables were lined with candles and carafes. The entire city was a spiced whirl of revelry and merriment in every nook and cranny, except one: the apartment directly opposite his own on the other side of the street.

It was eerily abandoned, the door gaping open wide.

Sitting, lulled by the salt-sea breeze the man thought he heard music, mesmerising music peeling out from those cracked black shutters. As he looked on, out stepped, in curves and curls, the most beautiful woman he had ever seen in his life. Her hair flowed down to her waist. Her dress was practically see-through. She looked straight at him. She blew him a kiss from her plush red lips.

Then he saw her skin was practically see-through. The flesh peeled down across her bones. Then, the orange blossoms in the window boxes burst into flame. In a flash of smoke and cinnamon, she vanished.

He awoke with a start, ran over to the balcony – nothing. The apartment over there, empty as before. Should he go over there? No that was a stupid idea.

Oh! There was someone there!

No. From the light of his own candle, it was just his shadow that nestled amongst the flowers across the street.

"Do you want to go in?" he asked his shadow, which gestured, "Here?"

"Yes," he nodded, "and tell me what's in there."

"Very well," the shadow seemed to nod.

He stood up, and his shadow stood up, because that is what shadows do.

He turned and his shadow turned, and he went into his room.
But the shadow did not follow him.

Next morning the young man stepped out on the balcony.
There was his coffee.
There was his pastry.
There was his notebook,
There was his –
"Where is my shadow?" he said.
It wasn't where it should be.
The first thing he felt was inspiration
"This is fantastic! This is exactly what I came here for."
He picked up his pen and he began to write, newly filled with fire and creative fury, stories of love, tales of loss. Then, as he wrote on, he remembered that he had heard many other stories about people losing their shadows. If he went home with this story, everyone would think he was copying them.
So he had to return home with nothing.
Not even a shadow.

Back up in the cold lands of the North, the young man persevered.
He wrote books about what was good in the world, what was beautiful and what was true.
Many years passed, and not much changed.
Until
Knock knock, said the door
"Who's there?" said the man
He saw a shiny black boot
A finely seamed trouser leg

A thick fur coat

A slender figure

A man in black who said, "Hello, old friend."

"Can I help you?" said the young man peering over his pile of notebooks.

He watched as the visitor removed his top hat. It was one of those really expensive new-fangled collapsible ones. He watched as the visitor scratched under a thick gold chain at his neck. He saw how every one of those black-gloved fingers was dripping in diamonds.

"Bless my soul," said the young man. "Who'd have thought a shadow could become a person? How did you come to be here, old friend?"

"You wanted me to tell you what I discovered in that room across the street."

"Oh, yes!" said the young man. "How faithful you are! Please sit yourself down. Tell me everything".

He sat, and the shadow sat. Because that's what shadows do.

"I will tell you what I found, but I want you to promise me something in return. I am thinking of finding a wife, and it would make things awkward if anyone were to know of my shadowy past. So you must promise not tell anyone I am a shadow."

"Of course!" said the young man. "We are old friends. You can trust me. I will tell not a soul. I promise on my life".

"Very well," said the shadow. "In that place I saw—"

"Yes?"

"I saw—"

"Yes?"

"I saw everything"

"Could you be a little more specific?"

"In that room I met poetry."

"Poetry! She must be the one I saw in my vision on the balcony. Oh she's often a recluse in the big cities. Oh, what did she reveal to you? The innocent words of the children at play? The soft romantic speeches of the lovers in the green hills? Or the divine inspiration of the priests in the holy shrines?"

"She showed me everything. She showed me the black thoughts in the bitter hearts of the priests in the holy shrines, the sugared deceptions of the lovers in the green hills, and the worst possible fate ahead for the innocent children at play, and how we use her to cover it all with her honeyed veil. She showed me *everything*.

What a place this world is. I wouldn't want to be human now, except it's the only thing to be. Had you gone in there, you wouldn't have become a man, but when I came out and you had gone, I was free to do what I wished with what she showed me.

"Had I worked for a newspaper I'd have made a lot of money, but instead I wrote to each individual that I met. I informed them that I knew beneath their carefully constructed layers of sugared artifice hid fragile thoughts and buried secrets. They were so afraid of me, they grew fond of me.

"Jewellers gave me gold, tailors gave me clothes, priests gave me blessings, professors gave me doctorates and women gave me attention. Favour by favour I raised myself up until I became the man you see before you today, and now – I'm on my way to a spa, want to come?"

"Oh. No. I'm busy. Still writing. Writing books, you remember? Good...truth...beauty?"

"Oh yes," said the shadow, sliding his finger over the bright white dust, "how's that going?"

42

"No one wants to read them really... or buy them... so I couldn't afford to come to a spa anyway."

"Well," said the shadow, "if it's a matter of money, if you came as my shadow, you could get in for free."

"Thank you," said the man.

"But I'd want you to promise me something in return. You must not tell anyone you are a man. It wouldn't be a very good disguise otherwise would it?"

The young man looked at his piles on piles of unsold books, at the cobwebs in the corners.

He decided it would be a good idea to travel.

But this time the shadow was the master of the man.

Trotting down the lane, the young man thought to make conversation with his old companion.

"My friend, now that you are a human being, you must have a name. Come on then, what is it? Let's be on familiar terms. Say *du* to me."

The shadow hissed, "As a poet I am sure you know human nature can be strange. When you invite me to say *du* to you this inexplicable, unpleasant feeling arises in me, like the sound of nails scraping on glass. Let's speak no more of it, shall we?"

They arrived at the spa, the springs and streams burbling with delight.

If the young man had thought the woman on the balcony was beautiful, he hadn't seen this one yet.

She floated softly through the crowd towards them, stopped in front of him, and said, "Hello, I am a princess, here being treated for the ailment of seeing things too clearly and I can see that you can't cast a shadow."

The young man had never had a person see him so clearly in his whole life. He opened his mouth, then remembered his promise. The shadow stepped forward,

"Your Highness, I think you will find you are wrong. Just as you have dressed your servants in fine uniforms, so I have dressed my shadow as a man. Doesn't he look good?"

"Oh, perhaps I do not see so clearly," said the princess. "Perhaps I have been cured!"

"Perhaps you have," said the shadow and he kissed her hand.

That night there was a celebration, held in honour of the princess's new-found health. She danced only with the shadow. He placed his strong arm around her slender waist, and her delicate hands in his thick black gloves, and he knew that she was falling in love with him, because she seemed to look straight through him.

Always in time, always one step behind, danced the man.

'This stranger looks as if he has done well for himself,' thought the princess, 'but a person needs more than wealth to be a man.'

So she asked him about philosophy, politics, history, and it seemed as if he knew everything.

'This is good,' she thought, 'but it takes more than knowledge for a man to be a husband.' So she asked him more questions. Questions about his journey through the world. Where he'd been, whom he'd met, what he'd seen. It seemed as if he had been everywhere and met everyone.

'This, too, is good,' she thought, 'but it takes more than experience for a husband to be a soul mate.' So she asked him more difficult questions. Questions about himself.

"Ha!" the shadow coughed, "these things! They are in such a deep part of me that even my shadow would know the answer to these questions. Why don't you ask him?" and he stepped to one side.

So, now the princess was looking into the eyes of the man. They sat. And they talked.

They talked all night about their innermost secrets and their outermost dreams, their deepest fears and their highest selves. About good, truth, beauty.

"If you are the shadow," said the princess, "what a man your master must be."

The young man opened his mouth.

And remembered his promise.

And watched in the early morning light as the princess announced to her entire entourage that she at last had met the tall dark handsome stranger of her dreams, and they would be married in her Golden City that night.

At the Golden City, behind the sapphire walls, in the silver guest lodgings the door slammed shut.

The shadow sat, and the man sat.

"After all your years of struggle. After all your years of pain and poverty in poetry, now at last you can live in luxury with me."

"Yes?" said the man, scribbling into his notebook.

"But I want you to promise me something in return. You mustn't tell anyone I'm a shadow, and you mustn't tell anyone you're a man."

"We've agreed that already," said the man.

"I haven't finished," said the shadow, and he tore the book out of the young man's hand and flung it on the fire. "You must never speak to anyone, ever again, and when I step out onto the balcony you must lie at my feet to prove exactly who you are to me."

"Oh no," said the young man, "this is too much, too far, I revoke my promise now."

"You have promised on your life," said the shadow.

"I don't care anymore," said the man, "you are asking me to sacrifice too much of myself. I will tell everyone. I will tell the King. I will tell the Queen. I will tell the beloved princess – you could never love that woman as I do – I will tell everyone. You are a shadow, I am the man."

"No one will believe you," said the shadow.

"I write about what's true," said the man.

"Yes, but no one reads your books."

The young man began to run, but shadows stretch so far and fast around this world that before he had reached anyone, he had been thrown in jail because everyone obeys the fiancé of a princess.

"You're shaking," the princess said, when the shadow stepped into the royal bedchamber. "You can't be sick now. It's our wedding night!"

"Can you believe it," he spat, "after everything I have done for him, my shadow went mad. Started spouting about being a man. I had to have him locked up."

"Oh how sad," said the princess. "You know, I have always seen things very clearly. When I spoke with him last night I did see that he was very troubled. Well, if it has come to this, perhaps we must remove him from his misery entirely."

The shadow uttered something that sounded like a sigh.

That night the shadow and the princess, newly married, stepped out on to the balcony as the people poured out onto the streets below. Fireworks exploded, trumpets blared. Tinkers, tailors, traders set up stalls. Tables were lined with candles and carafes. The entire city was a spiced whirl of merriment and revelry in every nook and cranny, except one.

The young man saw none of it because by then they had taken his life.

Hans Christian picks up the pen, trembling, the colour fading from his face and fantasies.
He writes:

Dear Edvard,

If only you could be with me in Italy, if only for a month.
If God had granted me to be a prince and you very poor, you would learn to appreciate me more than you do now. There is a place. I dream of it. After life. There I shall no longer be the destitute one. There we shall be equal.
Yours,

Andersen

Now as fast as his letter flies North, Hans Christian flies South, the journey as awkward as his long-limbed pace. Piling up cart-tracks, tunnels, mountains, country lanes and pilgrim pathways between himself and Edvard Collin, between reality and dream.

He takes out a fresh notebook. On the first page he writes

Oh to travel; to travel. If only one could spend a lifetime flitting from one place to another. And it would all be so much easier without a body – if one's spirit were free to go by itself.

On he goes, putting distance and paper between himself and Edvard Collin

To be in a strange haste with everything is my chief characteristic. Even in my travels it is not the present that pleases me. I hasten after something new, in order to come to something else. Every night when I lie down and rest I hanker after the next day and wish that it was here, and when it comes, it is still a distant future that occupies me. What am I hastening after?

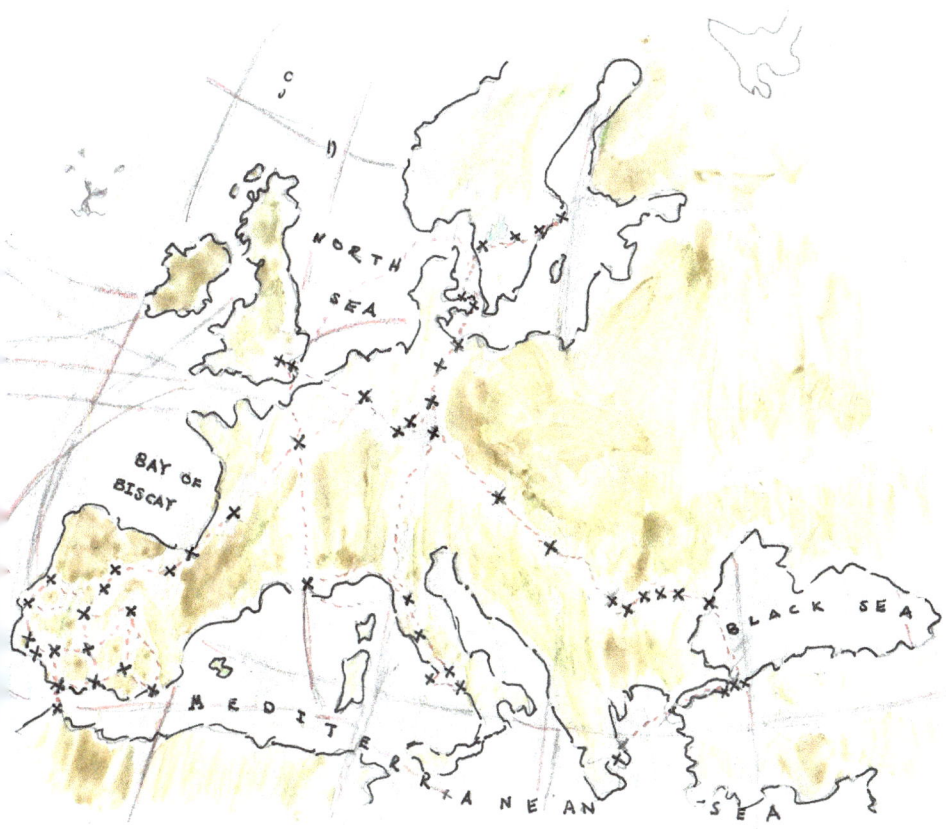

There is a place.

A forest. At night as dark as the place you find your-self when you shut your eyes.

In that forest sprang up one young fir tree.

In the searing heat of summer the seedling looked up, saw the sun and said, "I want that!" So, it began to climb. As it climbed it said, "What comes next? When will I be taller than the flowers? When will I be taller than the bushes? When will be taller than the tallest trees? When will I scrape the sky and spread my branches wide?"

"Enjoy your youth," said the sun as it passed overhead.

"Enjoy your fresh life," whispered the breeze, but the tree wasn't listening. It grew on and on, and one autumn day, after many autumn days that the tree had never noticed passing, it realised that it was just one needle's width from the height of the tallest trees.

"Yes!" it said, "Just one more needle, just one more!"

At that very moment, a group of men came into the forest, chopped down all the taller trees and carted them away.

"Oh," said the tree, "where did they go? What comes next?"

As they weren't there to answer for themselves, it had to ask the birds who nested in its branches.

"When we came back from our holiday in Egypt we saw your friends," the storks replied. "There on the oceans sail the great ships, and on the ships there are tall mast trees, who hold up the sails and guide the sailors home."

"Oh, to be trusted!" said the tree, "I want that!"

"We have seen your friends," the eagles said.

50

"When we fly over the hills and valleys we have seen them taken to a small place past the tall towers that puff clouds into the sky. In one end go your friends, and out they come, sliced in thin pieces, bound in leather, and the men say they are filled with wisdom."

"Oh, to be respected!" said the tree, "I want that!"

"But we," said the sparrows, "we have seen the finest thing of all. When we fly into the city in the middle of winter to collect our crumbs, we have seen your friends inside the people's houses. Surrounded, decorated, adored, and loved."

"Oh!" said the tree, "forget trust and respect! To be loved! Surely that is the most glorious path of all. When will that happen?"

It fell silent and put all of its labour into wishing and growing.

One crisp fresh winter's day, after many winter days it never noticed passing, a man trunched into the forest.

The man looked up.

The tree looked down.

"What comes next?" said the tree.

The man took out his axe.

He began to hack into the bark until it bit into the marrow. The tree stood defiant for a moment. Then, slow and steady, catapulted needles to the forest floor. Its branches tangled in the limbs of other trees as if trying still to stay upright, but no other tree was strong enough to hold its weight. The ring on ring on ring revealed how long it had been growing there. The sweet and sticky sap. The lifeless stump.

The tree was hauled onto a cart and taken to the city.

Amber lanterns reflected in the harbour ice. The tree could see how each house was aglow, as parlour by parlour was lit with the light of a hundred candles on every freshly cut fir tree.

The carriage pulled up in front of a grand house. The horses jangled to a stop and puffed steam into the air.

Out stepped the servants, who dragged the tree over the flagstone steps, down the hallway and into to a large room, where they set it in a bucket of soil.

There were portraits on the wall. Men and women. Men alone. Tall and proud like trees in a forest.

The servants looked up.

The tree looked down.

'What comes next?' thought the tree.

The servants began to decorate it. They tied red ribbons around it, wrapped it with gold and silver paper. They perfumed its bows with apples and cinnamon. Then they began to light the candles

'What comes next?' thought the tree.

'Will the birds fly past the window and recognise me? Will the trees from the forest come to admire me? Will I grow roots and stand here all winter and summer long?'

If trees could hyperventilate from excitement this tree would have hyperventilated, but they can't, they can only rustle.

So the tree rustled, set itself on fire, and one of the maids had to chuck water over it and they started all over again.

The door burst open.
In came children who gasped at its beauty.
Then they cried, "A story! A story!", and they pulled an old man over to sit at the foot of the tree.
"Very well," said the man, "since the tree has joined us tonight, I will tell you a story, but we only have time for one. Would you like the story of Clumpa Dumpa or Ickety Ackety?"
The man told the tale of Clumpa Dumpa (Do you know it? I'm sure you do. Clumpa Dumpa fell down the stairs, but still won the heart of the princess). This reminded the fir tree of a little silver birch it had grown past in the forest. Hadn't really noticed her at the time.
Then the children and the old man blew the candles out and left.

In the dark the tree had time to think, 'Tomorrow they will come back and decorate me again, and sit all around me, and I will hear the tale of Clumpa Dumpa again. Then I will hear the one about Ickety Ackety too, and this time I won't set myself on fire. No. Now I know what to do, I will get things perfectly right.'
The tree stood still and pensive all night long.

In the morning, the doors burst open.
The room flooded with light.
The servants looked up.

The tree looked down

'What comes next?' thought the tree.

The servants reached up and caressed its bows.

They held it tightly.

They pulled it down.

They took it up to the attic and there they left it.

'Oh!' thought the tree, 'what comes next?'

And it had plenty of time to wonder, because night and day and day and night no one came up to the attic except, scurrying through its branches, the mice.

"Hello old fir tree," they said.

"I am not old," it said, "I've just stopped growing."

"Tell us about yourself," they begged as they gathered around.

The tree began to speak. It told them about its childhood in the forest, its journey to the city, about the decorations, and it told them the story of Clumpa Dumpa. Because that was the only story it knew how to tell.

"What a lucky life you've lived," said the wide-eyed mice. "Every moment must be sheer pleasure."

They went to the parlour to eat cheese.

Now it was alone, the tree had time to think.

'Clumpa Dumpa fell down the stairs. Still won the heart of the princess. I got chopped down but – as the mice said – what a good and lucky life I have. When I get out will not take it for granted any longer. I will make the most of every moment, and never wonder about the next. I will get things perfectly right.'

One spring day after many spring days the tree never

noticed passing, the servants came back up to the attic. They tied ropes around its trunk, hooked those ropes onto a pulley, gave a shout, and pushed it out through a door in the roof.

It could feel the sun, the air, the wind, the dew

"Now!" the tree sang. "Anything is possible! Now, life can begin once more!"

And as it once had dreamed it scraped the sky and spread its branches wide.

They were brown and yellow and brittle.

"It's over," said the tree, "it's over."

As it dropped down it could see that there in the garden, the roses and the linden trees were in full bloom.

Then the man who had chopped the tree down in the forest came over, chopped it into pieces, made a neat stack and set it alight. How wonderfully it flared up under a copper cauldron. The children ran around, imitating the sounds it made.

Hiss,

Pop,

Crack,

Wheeze,

And every wheeze was a sigh and every sigh was a memory of a dappled morning as a tiny sapling in the forest, or the winter night when it finally got tall enough to see over the opposite hill, of the silver birch tree, and of Clumpa Dumpa, the only story it had ever heard, or known how to tell.

Before long the tree burned up, (though it smoldered on).
It was over.
And that's what happens to every story.

My ~~true~~
My ~~proper~~
My ~~actual~~
My ~~proper, actual~~
My ~~real~~
~~My~~

My current first love.
No really. Here we are now. All of us. You and me.

We met about eighteen months ago. In the first sixty seconds
of our meeting, I thought he looked so innocent he must be
fifteen.
But he isn't innocent.
(He isn't fifteen).
Somehow he has managed to preserve a thoughtful,
trustworthy soul in all of this mess.

So why are the bags in my room still half-packed?
What is the sign I am waiting for?
Should there be some swelling music to tell me it's the
finalé?
What comes next?

I can't get out of my mind the idea that there's a place –
there's always another place – there is a Place where I will
suddenly know enough to know that everything is right.
And we will lay down together in crisp white sheets, and
I will fall asleep beside him, deeply in love, safe in the
knowledge that one day our hearts will just open.

What a journey.

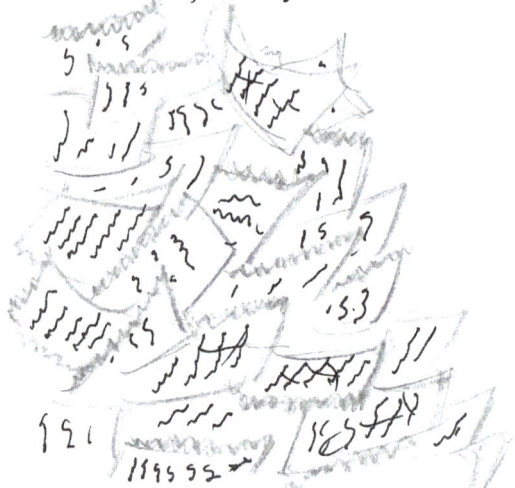

Look how far we've come.

There is a place.
A kitchen.
In the kitchen sat the possessions of an elegant gentleman: a boot-scraper, a comb and a collar.

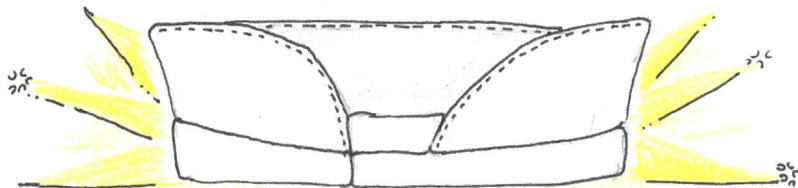

The collar had reached the age when he was thinking about falling in love and getting married, and he happened to land in the wash with the garter.

"Oh," said the collar, "I've never met anyone like you before. So slender, so elegant, so soft, so dainty."

"You shouldn't speak to me like that," said the garter, "I have given you no cause to."

"Oh yes," said the collar, "when someone is as lovely as you I can't help it. May I ask your name?"

"Do I even know you?" said the garter.

The collar was taken out of the wash, and hung on the chair to dry in the sun. Along came the iron to press him "Madam!", he exclaimed, "you are so hot! I can feel you un-crinkling all of my creases. I love y—"

"Shhhhhh!" said the iron as she passed overhead, imagining herself to be a great steam train on the iron railroad.

The collar was little frayed around the edges, so the scissors came along to snip him.

"Oh," said the collar, "look at your long shiny legs! You must be a dancer. What are you doing for the rest of your life?"

"Is he proposing?" the scissors thought. She was so cross that she snipped at him until he had to be thrown in the bin.

"Oh," sighed the collar, looking at himself. "Now, I suppose I shall have to marry the comb.

"It's, uhm, remarkable how you've kept all your teeth, little Miss. Have you ever thought about getting married?"

"Oh, yes!" said the comb. "I am engaged to the boot-scraper".

Now there was no one left to marry, the collar felt only contempt for the whole idea.

A long time passed and the collar ended up in the rag bin at a paper mill.

There was a big rag party there. All of the rags had plenty to talk about, but the collar spoke most of all.

"I have had a great many loves," he said.

"My first love was soft, so elegant, so dainty. Threw herself in the wash for my sake. What could I do but move on? But my *real* first love – phew – she was hot! I'm telling you, too hot for me! Couldn't handle it! Had to get out of there. What could I do but move on? But my *proper*, my *genuine*, my real first love was a dancer who gave me the scars I now bear. But my *actual*, my proper, my real, my true, my – my current first love is a comb who's waiting for me at home, totally lovesick. Yes, I have this all on my conscience, it's about time I was turned into a fresh sheet of paper and given another chance."

That is just what happened.

Well, all the rags were turned into paper.
But the collar was turned into the piece of paper on which this story is written.

And as open as we think we keep ourselves, we never know when our story will imprint itself on us anyway. Our whole story, even our innermost secrets, set down and clear for everyone to see, and then we'll have to run around talking about it, just like the collar.

Well, all the rags were turned into paper
But the collar was turned into the piece of paper on which this Story is written.

And as open as ve think we keep ourselves, we never know when our story will imprint itself on us anyway. Our whole story, even our innermost secrets, set down and clear for everyone to see, and then we'll have to run around talking about it, just like the collar.

Wedding bells are ringing clear and true in the heaving summer air. The pews are lined with crinolines, the new fashion crowding the cathedral.

In the dappled light of a stained glass window, the man with steel-blue eyes lifts the veil of the woman kneeling beside him. They make their vows and leave in bright sunshine, the cheers of friends and family heralding their happy life ahead.

To the East, a man with pale white skin and pea-green eyes sits curled in perspiration over the impatient paper, trying to ignore the wedding invitation stuck through on the wall with a sharp brass tack.

He writes:

My dear and faithful Edvard.

If you looked down to the bottom of my soul, you would understand fully the source of my longing, and pity me. The open transparent waters have depths that even divers do not know, yet you and I will never speak of it.
Like Moses I stand on a mountain, looking into a land that I will never reach –

He lifts the pen and contemplates the page.
Holds it up to the light.
Tears it away.
Starts again.

My dear Edvard,

God bless you both and go with you. Indeed you will be happy and you deserve it.

Andersen

He lifts the pen and contemplates the page. Neatly folds the letter over twice.

He looks out of the window and sees a man and woman walking arm in arm along the shore.
Watches the nesting birds wheeling through the the sky in pairs.
He wishes he could be more like Edvard. Keep his emotions safely in check, preserved for only the most appropriate of uses.

How do you do that?

He shuts his eyes.
For a moment he remembers sitting in a corner of a classroom, with the teacher sat high up on her chair, and she opened the old book of fairytales and she read...
He looks down at the empty paper
He picks up the pen.
He writes:

There is a place

And once he starts writing, maybe you know how it is? He can't seem to stop. It all pours out.

...the little mermaid pulled back the purple drapes of the tent. She looked at the sleeping prince, and – resting in his arms – the beautiful princess. She looked up at the sky, where the light of dawn was glowing stronger and stronger. She fixed her eyes once more on the prince, who, in his dreams, called out his bride's name. She was the only one in his thoughts. There was no hope now. She flung her dagger far out to sea where the waves rippled red like blood.

One more time with eyes half-glazed she looked at him.

Then she threw herself from the ship to the sea, and she felt her body turning into foam on the ocean waves.

Acknowledgements & Notes

Thanks to Anthony Alderson, Clive Birnie, Bridget Hart, Phillip Breen, Kath Burlinson, Cassandra Mathers, Pippa & Derek Reid, Ben Reizenstein, Ben Monks and Will Young (Supporting Wall), Joel Stanley, Naomi West.

Recommended reading:
Hans Christian Andersen: The Life of a Storyteller; Jackie Wullschläger (Penguin)
Hans Christian Andersen: The Fan Dancer; Allison Prince (Allison & Busby)
Fairy Tales by Hans Christian Andersen, translated by Tiina Nunally, edited and introduced by Jackie Wullschläger (Penguin Classics)

Lightning Source UK Ltd.
Milton Keynes UK
UKHW051846291121
394796UK00003B/6